The
SURRENDERED LIFE

The SURRENDERED LIFE

A PEARL OF IMMENSE VALUE

TABITHA HENTON LAMB

Contents

Note From Author

My authorship in this publication is in no way meant to leave the impression I have arrived. It is my assignment as a messenger to deliver His word. I write cloaked in humility and covered in grace. Blessings!

Introduction

The kingdom of heaven is like unto a merchant man, seeking goodly pearls: Who, when he had found one pearl of great price, went and sold all that he had, and bought it (Matthew 13:45-46).

This is a parable of a man in search of something very rare and of great value. Upon finding this matchless pearl, the man sells all that he has to acquire this extravagant piece. We too when we discover the surpassing riches in Christ, are prepared to give up all other attachments to enjoy the greatest treasure of all.

This book is all about pursuing our reward in Christ. But it is also about the things that hold us back and vie for our attention. We all wish to lay hold of the life destined for us in God, but we must first weigh in on a subject that is difficult to come to grips with. It is the sinful nature or the self life. We must become aware of its nature and its progressive working against us in our desire and ability to achieve true sonship.

But like anything of value there is a price. Didn't Jesus say, *"For which of you, intending to build a tower, sitteth not down first, and counteth the cost, whether he have sufficient to finish it?"* (Luke 14:28). So must we consider what is working against us as we move towards our purpose.

We have the assurance of Jesus that this purpose is within our reach, and it is attainable. But we must follow the same instruction Jesus gave to the father of the boy with the deaf and dumb spirit, *"If thou canst believe, all things are possible to him that believeth"* (Mark 9:23). So are all things we wish to attain through faith.

At the outset of this spiritual voyage we will discover some hard but binding truths. But be comforted that what the Holy Spirit reveals, He also heals. He is both gracious and longsuffering. With Him comes the conviction that leads to repentance and to righteousness. Anything outside of this stray into the path of condemnation, which leads to fear and judgment.

So let us believe that the Word does not seek to condemn but to save:

> *For God so loved the world, that he gave his only begotten Son, that whosoever believeth in him should not perish, but have everlasting life, For*

God sent not his Son into the world to condemn the world; but that the world through him might be saved. He that believeth on him is not condemned: but he that believeth not is condemned already because he hath not believed in the name of the only begotten Son of God. And this is the condemnation, that light is come into the world, and men loved darkness rather than light, because their deeds were evil (John 3:16-19).

In this exposition, we will contrast the works of the flesh with those of the Spirit. We will take stock not only of every blessing and setback in our lives but also the schemes of the enemy that are so glaring and real. Make no mistake; he comes with only one intention: to kill, to steal and to destroy. Whether or not we choose to accept this as true, it does not qualify the reality of demonic influence. One can choose either the path of truth, which is light, or the path of continued deception, which is darkness.

*But if we **walk** in the light, as he is **in** the light, we have fellowship one with another, and **the** blood of Jesus Christ his Son cleanseth us from all sin (1 John 1:7, emphasis added).*

We know Jesus has already paid the ultimate price for all we will unveil. We therefore need to commit to understanding and equipping ourselves with the foundational truths expounded in this book and hold them close to our hearts. The primary one is to abandon a lifestyle of sin:

> *He that committeth sin is of the devil; for the devil sinneth from the beginning. For this purpose the Son of God was manifested, that he might destroy the works of the devil"* (1 John 3:8).

> *For the wages of sin is death; but the gift of God is eternal life through Jesus Christ our LORD* (Romans 6:23).

If you have read beyond this introduction, it is a sign you wholeheartedly seek more of God and less of self. You have arrived at a frame of mind to accept all scripture as revealed concerning the self life and you aspire to go beyond life as circumscribed by self.

For those seeking more, we know that because of Jesus and the work of the Holy Spirit, we can move into all the Father has made possible in sending His Son. Join me in this journey towards a deeper life in Christ. Know that the journey culminates in absolute surrender to His will, no longer to yours. Engage in the pursuit with a mindset of discovering and understanding. Say to yourself, "I must go this way to acquire my true objective, which is sonship."

Before we begin we must assess by all means necessary whatever it takes to become sons. It will require a strong commitment and unyielding determination; however, the rewards will be glorious. So this is my prayer for you:

> *That he would grant you, according to the riches of his glory, to be strengthened with might by his Spirit in the inner man; That Christ may dwell in your hearts by faith; that ye, being rooted and grounded in love, May be able to comprehend with all saints what is the breadth, and length, and depth, and height; And to know the love of Christ, which passeth knowledge with all the fulness of God. Now unto him that is able to do exceeding abundantly above all that we ask or think, according to the power that worketh in us, Unto him be glory in the church by Christ Jesus throughout all ages, world without end. Amen* (Ephesians 3:16-21).

Chapter 1

The Whole Duty of Man

The word of God commands us to love the Lord our God with all our heart, with all our soul, with all our might, and to love our neighbor as ourselves (Matthew 22:37).

The whole duty of humankind towards their Maker is one of obedience out of a love relationship. This is what Jesus came to show us where Adam failed. Adam and Eve chose to take their own path, loving themselves above God. That act of betrayal meant many things: attempting to usurp His wisdom and knowledge, abdicating dominion over the earth, refusing to love Him with all of their heart, soul and might, and becoming self-seeking souls. In short it meant, robbing God of the beauty of what He created, and the purpose for which creation exists.

Adam and Eve chose to see life from their own perspective, and to use it to serve themselves and not God and others. Like opportunists they chose to lavish what they had received upon themselves. Little did they realize God's command was a test of the heart to see if they would remain under the protection and care of the Omniscient God through obedience to Him.

The command was a simple yet profound one: not to eat of the Tree of the Knowledge of Good and Evil. All it required of them was to receive this command and obey it. The ability to do so is determined by the motives and intents of the heart. Regardless of the words of our mouth, our true nature lies in our heart. Adam and Eve set their hearts on being disobedient. They chose to serve themselves when all creation around them revolved around the One who created them. The knowledge they took for themselves did not belong to them. It was a truly malicious crime of robbery of trust in the heart which produced the nature of inbred sin. That act resulted in this downward spiral of the quality of life bequeathed to all humanity.

Jesus came to show us the exact opposite. This kingdom that He came to reveal is what some would call "an upside-down kingdom," with the One at the top, God, serving the best interests of all. On our part we are to love God with all of who we are and to love our neighbor as we love ourselves. We can see that the kingdom of man and of Satan are the polar opposite to the Kingdom of God. These are self-seeking kingdoms whose whole obligation is to love ourselves with all of our heart, soul and might. This is why we have such a kindred spirit with the kingdom of darkness and why the nature of man so closely mirrors that of Satan and not God. This is the result of the fall of humankind after Satan deceived Eve in the garden.

So, equally by deception, we have received that fallen legacy. We are now in his territory, and cannot match him in his cunning, ability, and deceitful craft. In our endeavor to seek our own independence and be apart from God, we have unknowingly joined forces with Satan himself. You see, the devil knows the individual disposition of each person. He will wage a spiritual war against each of us according to what he knows will be the best way to keep each person from reconnecting with his Creator. His demons constantly wage war on the saints to feed them with false concepts about God and to make them weak. They do their utmost to keep us in poverty and failures so as to keep them powerless, and bring reproach upon God and His Gospel.

Satan will stop at nothing to gain his ends. He has no righteous principle about him and has no respect for either God or man. He is out to defeat man through his vulnerabilities. In some respects He has a distinct advantage as men have inherited the sinful nature and are spiritually dead. Humanity is born with a propensity to live in sin and selfishness.

So as a result of the fall, humanity is birthed contrary to God's thoughts and ways, and cannot conform to them through their own reasoning and effort. The carnal mind is not subject to the laws of God, neither can it be. It cannot understand the ways of God.

> *For my thoughts are not your thoughts neither are your ways my ways, saith the Lord. For as the heavens are higher than the earth so are my ways higher than your ways, and my thoughts than your thoughts* (Isaiah 55:8-9).

The core impediment to entering the kingdom of heaven is the selfish nature of man. Its duty is to serve himself by any means necessary, with no real purpose outside of himself.

By contrast, the original purpose of man is wrapped in man's whole duty. When you love someone as you love yourself, you have the duty to love despite their deeds or offenses. If we had this mindset, here is where we extend the same grace we have for ourselves to those outside. In other words, when you love the way God loves, your love reflects His generous character. His goodness rains upon both the just and the unjust. He is merciful, kind, and gracious to the righteous and the unrighteous. He goes to the same great lengths to save the sinner as He does to protect the one who is in right standing with Him. And when the sinner comes to Him, He rejoices with all of Heaven in a great celebration. He hates sin but He loves the sinner and the righteous alike.

On the other hand, the Pharisees, the scribes, the Sanhedrin, the priests, the Jews, failed to see the graciousness of God. Their hearts had become conditioned to the letter of the law and not the true intent and spirit of the law. This is what John came to reveal: to prepare the heart of man to receive the kingdom. And what was his message? Repentance from the heart. The kingdom of heaven was at hand, but outside of true repentance they would not enter this kingdom.

In this Kingdom sat a King whose heart was tender toward the Jews and extended His mercy to all of humankind. However, the religious leaders were looking for a self-seeking kingdom which served their interests only. They could not see the kingdom Jesus came to establish because they misunderstood prophesy. They were looking for a kingdom that would come and overthrow the Romans who were governing them.

How do we enter the kingdom of heaven? Jesus told Nicodemus in John 3 that unless a man is "born again," he cannot see the kingdom of heaven. He must be born of the Spirit and Water to go beyond physical sight. The flesh and the human spirit can only produce after their own kind. But the spirit filled with God rises above the spirit dominated by the flesh. Just as the wind blows, you cannot see the wind of the Spirit, but you can hear it. It is an affair of the heart.

Therefore the kingdom of heaven cannot be seen by those whose heart is set on themselves and their own agenda. It cannot be accessed until one has had a complete change of heart. That is why the Pharisees were unable to see it. They wanted to take the benefits of what God made available to them but retain the independence of a self-seeking life. This could not remain forever without eternal consequences.

When the blind man was healed Jesus told the Pharisee's they were blind because, if they were not, they would be able to see the kingdom of heaven. They argued they were not blind because they had placed their security in the law of Moses. Note Jesus' response, *"If you were blind, you would have no sin; but now you say, 'We see.' Therefore your sin remains"* (Matthew 9:41 NKJV).

God gives power and wealth so that His Kingdom will be established here on earth. It is not until we seek only the Glory, Honor, and Approval of God that we can be trusted with the kingdom of heaven and all its resources and power. The reason we cannot be trusted with the goodness of God and the resources of His Kingdom is because we will use it to bring reproach upon God. In our quest for possession, power and vain glory, we will use our resources to serve ourselves, and ultimately Satan, as this was his mission when he tried to dethrone God.

No wonder we walk around defeated and see so much death and destruction around us! We have settled comfortably into a form of godliness, denying His power as it would cause us to separate ourselves from the kingdoms of this world. We find this difficult because we care only about serving ourselves and any other who is pursuing the same goals.

Now we come to this chilling truth. There will be those operating ostensibly in the kingdom of heaven who will not enter the Kingdom of God. He will say, "Depart from Me for, I never knew you. You were not ever my own even though you worked in my kingdom. You offered service but not your heart. Even though you say, 'I healed in your name, rendered service, and worked in your kingdom,' the judgment is the same as one who is classified as a sinner. So depart from Me – I never knew you, you workers of iniquity" (see Matthew 7:22-23).

Chapter 2

The Spirit of Rebellion

We just discussed how we lost sight of our duty towards God due to our self-seeking nature. In this pursuit we developed Man Consciousness versus God Consciousness. Man consciousness was not our inherited nature but an adopted one. This was not the original intent but somehow, we bought into the deception that we could be our own gods.

We conduct our lives as we see fit, content with living a life outside of a realm not intended for us. Let us assess what we find in this realm. Then let us look to see what we find in the realm of God Consciousness. This requires that we understand our intended purpose from the beginning and how we bought into the misconception of something we assumed to be true without properly investigating the truth.

Let us look again at Adam and Eve's approach, which was motivated by rebellion, and pride and search our hearts for a different approach. If only we could go back to the original intent! Oh what truth our hearts will come to know, what fulfillment our souls will come to rest in! What healing and wholeness will lavish themselves over our body! What an awakening of our spirits that would be!

According to Genesis 1:26, God in His triune being, made man (male and female) in His own image and likeness. After He created them, He blessed them and put them in a home that was prepared for them. Man was told to replenish (put back what was lost), to cultivate, to keep and preserve, guard and protect that domain from all intruders.

God then commissioned man to have dominion over the air, the land, and the sea – (the fowl, the cattle, the creepers, and the fish). All this He did in the realm of God Consciousness. Unknown to the man there was a world that had existed before him as described in Genesis chapter 1:1-2:

> *In the beginning God created the heaven and the*
> *earth. And the earth was without form, and void;*
> *and darkness was upon the face of the deep.*

This verse tells us that the earth of the original creation was in a state of chaos. 2 Peter 3:5-7 reveals a world standing out of the water and in the water before it was flooded with water and perished.

However, in the second part of Genesis 1:2 we read: *"And the Spirit of God moved upon the face of the waters ..."* waiting for the timing of a restoration process. Let us find out why a restoration process was necessary. What caused the first creation to be in chaos we ask?

In Luke 10:18, Jesus refers to the overthrow of Satan from heaven: *"I beheld Satan as lightning fall from heaven."* Satan or Lucifer had fallen from heaven. He was the son of the morning! He who weakened the nations was cut down to the ground! Why was this so? Because he said in his heart,

> *I will ascend into heaven, I will exalt my throne*
> *above the stars of God: I will also sit upon the*
> *mount of the congregation, in the sides of the north:*
> *I will ascend above the heights of the clouds; I will*
> *be like the highest* (Isaiah 14:12-15).

Satan's downfall is again referred to in Ezekiel 28. It starts off with the king of Tyrus (Tyre) and shifts to Lucifer. Here we see the law of double mention in operation. In this law a visible person is addressed, but an invisible person, who is using the visible person as a tool, is implied. So the king of Tyrus' evil deeds recall Lucifer and his rebellion.

The passage shows a conversation between God and Ezekiel, where Ezekiel is told to speak a lamentation upon the King of Tyrus:

> *Son of man, take up a lamentation upon the king*
> *of Tyrus, and say unto him, Thus saith the Lord*

God; Thou sealest up the sum, full of wisdom, and perfect in beauty.

Thou hast been in Eden the garden of God; every precious stone was thy covering, the sardius, topaz, and the diamond, the beryl, the onyx, and the jasper, the sapphire, the emerald, and the carbuncle, and gold: the workmanship of thy tabrets and of thy pipes was prepared in thee in the day that thou wast created.

Thou art the anointed cherub that covereth; and I have set thee so: thou wast upon the holy mountain of God; thou hast walked up and down in the midst of the stones of fire.

Thou wast perfect in thy ways from the day that thou wast created, till iniquity was found in thee.

By the multitude of thy merchandise they have filled the midst of thee with violence, and thou hast sinned: therefore I will cast thee as profane out of the mountain of God: and I will destroy thee, O covering cherub, from the midst of the stones of fire.

*Thine heart was lifted up because of thy beauty,
thou hast corrupted thy wisdom by reason of thy
brightness: I will cast thee to the ground, I will lay
thee before kings, that they may behold thee.*

*Thou hast defiled thy sanctuaries by the multitude
of thine iniquities, by the iniquity of thy traffick;
therefore will I bring forth a fire from the midst of
thee, it shall devour thee, and I will bring thee to
ashes upon the earth in the sight of all them that
behold thee.*

*All they that know thee among the people shall
be astonished at thee: thou shalt be a terror, and
never shalt thou be any more* (Ezekiel 28:12-19).

Let us recount Jeremiah's vision in chapter 4:23-26, which gives us a very vivid assessment of the aftermath of Lucifer's act of rebellion.

*I beheld the earth, and, lo, it was without form,
and void; and the heavens, and they had no light.
I beheld the mountains, and, lo, they trembled,
and all the hills moved lightly. I beheld, and, lo,
there was no man, and all the birds of the heavens
were fled. I beheld, and, lo, the fruitful place was*

*a wilderness, and all the cities thereof were broken
down at the presence of the LORD, and by his fierce
anger.*

So God in His wrath destroyed His first creation. Genesis 1:2 shows the Spirit of God hovering over the waters as if planning His next move, and the rest of the chapter records the recreation of the universe after it had been destroyed by His own hand.

There is a price to pay for rebellion and we shall see the consequences in man.

Chapter 3

The Self Life

n this chapter we will see how the self life started out in the garden.

And the Lord God took the man and put him into the garden of Eden to dress it and to keep it. And the Lord God commanded the man, saying, Of every tree of the garden thou mayest freely eat: But of the tree of the knowledge of good and evil, thou shalt not eat of it: for in the day that thou eatest thereof thou shalt surely die (Genesis 2:15-17).

*And the serpent said unto the woman, Ye shall not surely die: For God doth know that in the day ye eat thereof, then your eyes shall be opened, and ye shall be as gods, knowing good and evil. And when the woman saw that the tree was **good for food**, and that it was **pleasant to the eyes**, and a tree to be desired to **make one wise**, she took of the fruit thereof, and did eat, and gave also unto her husband with her; and he did eat (Genesis 3:4-6, emphasis added).*

What enticed Eve to partake of the fruit were three things: good for food, pleasant to the eyes, and capable of making one wise. These three elements are summed up as the world's temptations in 1 John 2:16:

> *For all that is in the world, the lust of the flesh,*
> *and the lust of the eyes, and the pride of life, is not*
> *of the Father, but is of the world.*

So the devil tempted Eve to eat of the fruit by appealing to her senses (lust of the flesh), her perceptions (lust of the eyes), and self-glory (pride of life). In effect these three components have become the lure of the world system. We will expand on each one further. However, first, we will define the word "lust."

Lust is an emotional force producing intense desire for something even though we may already have a significant amount of it. It can take any form such as lust for sex, money, or power, or even more mundane forms as the lust for food – as distinct from the need for food – or lust for idleness. Lust is different from passion, in that passion can propel individuals to achieve benevolent goals. But lust is an insatiable overwhelming desire or craving for anything sinful and contrary to the will of God.

We are often deceived by our human nature; however,

God is not. We want Him to live by our deception rather than for us to live up to the standard of holiness. We had rather believe in our corrupt nature that denies us of true sonship. This corrupt nature produces sinful lust, which is an overpowering desire for what God has forbidden. As Apostle James warns us in 1 James 2:15, *"Love not the world, neither the things that are in the world. If any man love the world, the love of the Father is not in him."* All these temporal lusts will pass away and those that continue in them. *"And the world passeth away, and the lust thereof: but he that doeth the will of God abideth for ever"* (1 John 2:17).

Now let us examine these three lusts in greater detail.

The Lust of the Flesh

The lust of the flesh is everything that appeals to our carnal and sensual appetite. The root of the cravings is sensual gratification. The flesh is our human nature corrupted by sin so that our life is dominated by the senses. This also extends to being lax in moral values, selfish in the use of possessions, extravagant in the satisfaction of material desires. In a word, all these desires are centered in our fleshly nature with no care or concern for the will of God.

It is the flesh that constantly fights against the will of

God in our lives. It is contrary in nature to God's moral and spiritual laws. It does not relish the things of God and neither can it. It seeks only to live by its own rights – the self life. Those of us who continue to love the things of the world and who give ourselves over to the lust of the flesh are ready to be delivered into the hands of the world and to Satan.

But Paul instructs us to *"clothe yourself with the presence of the Lord Jesus Christ. And don't let yourself think about ways to indulge your evil desire"* (Romans 13:14 NLT).

The Lust of the Eyes

The lust of the eyes when we have a visual attraction is what incites covetousness, jealousy, or sexual lust. As fleshly creatures in a fallen world, natural wholesome desires can quickly become sinful lusts. Now not all desires are sinful in themselves such as the desire for food, water, shelter, security, belonging and comfort. However, since we are born with a sinful nature, our natural propensity is to satisfy ourselves and go beyond our basic needs. When this rules, it causes us to violate God's righteousness. When simple hunger becomes lust for food, it turns into gluttony.

Part of the reason Eve listened to the serpent in the Garden was that she looked at the forbidden fruit and saw that it was "pleasing to the eye." Satan used a visual image to entrap her. The greedy longing of the mind is the lust of the eye. It describes someone who is captivated by an outward show of materialism to covet the things it promises. It is a desire to have people, possessions, or status, to crave things which are outside our boundaries and against the will of God. This includes an inordinate lust for money, possessions, or fame.

Satan uses external attraction to produce covetousness through the eye. Just as the eye is the primary organ of perception, it is also the principal organ of temptation.

> *The light of the body is the eye: if therefore thine eye be single, thy whole body shall be full of light. But if thine eye be evil, thy whole body shall be full of darkness. If therefore the light that is in thee be darkness, how great is that darkness!* (Matthew 6:20-22)

The Pride of Life

Eve saw that the fruit was "a tree to be desired to make one wise..." – that is the pride of life. Consider Jesus' warnings about such a deadly sin in the parable of the rich man.

And he said unto them, Take heed, and beware of covetousness: for a man's life consisteth not in the abundance of the things which he possesseth.

And he spake a parable unto them, saying, The ground of a certain rich man brought forth plenti-fully: And he thought within himself, saying, What shall I do, because I have no room where to bestow my fruits? And he said, This will I do: I will pull down my barns, and build greater; and there will I bestow all my fruits and my goods. And I will say to my soul, Soul, thou hast much goods laid up for many years; take thine ease, eat, drink, and be merry. But God said unto him, Thou fool, this night thy soul shall be required of thee: then whose shall those things be, which thou hast provided? So is he that layeth up treasure for himself, and is not rich toward God (Luke 12:16-21).

The pride of life can therefore be described as total re-liance on one's own resources or stability in earthly things. Jesus tells us that these are transient and corruptible things:

Lay not up for yourselves treasures upon earth, where moth and rust doth corrupt, and where thieves break through and steal: For where your treasure is, there will your heart be also (Matthew 6:19-20).

In essence, the pride of life is the desire in every human being to be his or her own god. It is everything that appeals to haughtiness, arrogance, and pride. Here Satan uses personal achievement, popularity, or academic success to produce a self-sufficient persona. Everything we desire to have, to enjoy, or to pride ourselves with, this is the pride of life from sensuality and self-indulgence to self-conceit, ungodly gratification of appetites, mental self-satisfaction to egotistic arrogance. False views of pleasure, false views of possession, false views of superiority are also the pride of life. While the flesh does the lusting, it is the pride that glorifies the sin. "I am who I am because of me not because of God."

This is a dangerous place to be in. There can be no competition for His Glory. Regardless of how much He loves us and what He has done for us, the one thing He will not share is His Glory and His Praise. We must empty ourselves of all self-glory and the need for it, for it is the progenitor of all evil. We must reflect the Glory of God in our very nature and essence.

Jesus Overcame the 3 Lusts

Jesus shows us show we can overcome these core lusts by modeling how to stand up to Satan's temptations in the wilderness.

> *And when the tempter came to him, he said, If*
> *thou be the Son of God, command that these stones*
> *be made bread* (Matthew 4:3).

First, Satan tried to tempt Jesus by the lust of the flesh when he urged him to turn the stones into bread. He tried to get Him to satisfy His own personal hunger after a long fast by a very wholesome commodity – bread. But the issue here was not about eating, but about accepting the enemy's suggestion instead of being dependent upon God for His every need.

What was Jesus response? *"It is written, Man shall not live by bread alone, but by every word that proceedeth out of the mouth of God"* (verse 4).

Spiritual bread as defined here by Jesus is vitally important to us. The word of God was His weapon in defeating the trap of Satan. In other words, He was saying, "I am not responding to your challenge to prove my identity. I know who I am and who My Provider is. I do not have to give a demo for your sake."

It isn't that Jesus was against eating because he ate the food the angels brought him when the trial was over (Matthew 4:11). What was important was in submitting to His Father's timing and will in all things. In this Jesus demonstrated victory over the fleshly nature.

The second temptation concerned the lust of the eye.

> *Then the devil taketh him up into the holy city, and setteth him on a pinnacle of the temple, And saith unto him, If thou be the Son of God, cast thyself down: for it is written, He shall give his angels charge concerning thee: and in their hands they shall bear thee up, lest at any time thou dash thy foot against a stone.*
>
> *Jesus said unto him, It is written again, Thou shalt not tempt the Lord thy God* (Matthew 4:5-7).

Here we see the devil urging Him to do some spectacular miracle again to prove He was the Son of God. Doing that would be an act of disobedience, for Jesus only did what He heard the Father tell Him to do. What is interesting is that the devil was quoting Psalm 91, when the word clearly says that God's total protection is implicit for all those that "dwell in the *secret place* of the Most High God." It's a private place, not one for show.

In the third temptation we find the pride of life being waved at Jesus.

> *Again, the devil taketh him up into an exceeding high mountain, and sheweth him all the kingdoms of the world, and the glory of them; And saith unto him, All these things will I give thee, if thou wilt fall down and worship me* (Matthew 4:8-9).

The devil appealed to Jesus using the pride of life tactic when he showed Him all the kingdoms of the world and their glory. "All these things will I give You if You will fall down and worship me," he said. Satan used a powerful visual – all the kingdoms of the world and their splendor – when he offered Jesus an opportunity to rule the world with Him. Now note that since the fall, Satan had taken dominion over all the kingdoms of the earth through man's abdication of his position. Jesus was aware of that and did not contest it. But He also knew God's perfect timing when all the kingdoms of the earth would be the kingdoms of His Son (Revelation 11:15).

So what was His response? "*Then saith Jesus unto him, Get*

thee hence, Satan: for it is written, Thou shalt worship the Lord thy God, and him only shalt thou serve" (verse 10).

Jesus was saying, "I bow to know one except to My God!" Here was the devil trying to tempt Him with what was already His as God. What could he show Him that would cause the Son of God to fall down and worship him? What a pathetic attempt to challenge the One who was there since the very beginning and caused the creation of everything (including Lucifer)!

John 1:1-3 tells us,

> *In the beginning was the Word, and the Word was with God, and the Word was God. The same was in the beginning with God. All things were made by him; and without him was not anything made that was made. And the Word was made flesh, and dwelt among us, (and we beheld his glory, the glory as of the only begotten of the Father,) full of grace and truth.*

In these temptations we find the true agenda of Satan. It was not what he was trying to get Jesus to do but why he was trying to get Jesus to succumb to his temptations. He wanted Jesus to doubt His identity as Son of God. These are the same strategies that Satan still uses on us today: to cause us to lose our identity as sons of the living God and new creations in Christ. When we do that, we succumb to the lust of the flesh, the lust of the eye and the pride of life. We choose the kingdoms of this world and all their pleasures over the kingdom of God.

How do we overcome these temptations? By following Jesus' example as a man – using the power of His Word. In each one of these situations Jesus chose to honor His Father more than to honor Himself. He used the Word of God as His weapon to defeat the lies of Satan and overcome temptation. We are to know and to desire Jesus and the power of His resurrection in such a way that we too honor Him and are empowered by His Word.

In this we desire nothing more than the fellowship of sharing in His sufferings. Our eyes are set on Jesus. Our view is to eternity. Our very existence is Him. We chose to live a life crucified with Christ so that we may live unto the Glory of God. Those of us who continue to seek after the will of God will see the fruit of the Spirit manifesting in our lives.

In the process, we come to discover who we are in Him. To live without things, people, or relationships we can do; however, to live or to fathom a life without Christ we cannot.

For God, who commanded the light to shine out of darkness, hath shined in our hearts, to give the light of the knowledge of the glory of God in the face of Jesus Christ. But we have this treasure in earthen vessels, that the excellency of the power may be of God, and not of us (2 Corinthians 4:6-8).

If we continue to be drawn by the lust of the eyes, the lust of the flesh and the pride of life, it is impossible to do the will of God and to inherit eternal life. We can claim to be Christian but didn't Jesus warn us: *"Not every one that saith unto me, Lord, Lord, shall enter into the kingdom of heaven; but he that doeth the will of my Father which is in heaven"* (Matthew 7:21)?

My heart is so heavy for those who do not know Him. God, send laborers across Your vineyard today to minster to the hearts of those who have not come to know You through Your Son Jesus.

Chapter 4

Self Love

elf love can be defined as "love of self" or "regard for one's own happiness or advantage." It can start off as a basic human necessity. But it can escalate into a moral flaw, akin to vanity and selfishness, and is synonymous with *amour-propre*, conceitedness, egotism, and even narcissism.

Of course, self-preservation the first law of human nature but it is not the first law from God. Let us become familiar with God's purpose for love. We find this in a conversation between Jesus and one of the scribes in Mark 12:28-34:

> *And one of the scribes came, and having heard them reasoning together, and perceiving that he had answered them well, asked him, Which is the first commandment of all?*
>
> *And Jesus answered him, The first of all the commandments is, Hear, O Israel; The Lord our God is one Lord: And thou shalt love the Lord thy God with all thy heart, and with all thy soul, and with all thy mind, and with all thy strength: this is the first commandment. And the second is*

like, namely this, Thou shalt love thy neighbour as thyself. There is none other commandment greater than these.

And the scribe said unto him, Well, Master, thou hast said the truth: for there is one God; and there is none other but he: And to love him with all the heart, and with all the understanding, and with all the soul, and with all the strength, and to love his neighbour as himself, is more than all whole burnt offerings and sacrifices.

And when Jesus saw that he answered discreetly, he said unto him, Thou art not far from the kingdom of God.

Jesus prioritized the love of God and the love others above our own needs or wants. In fact, Paul the Apostle in his letter to the Philippians wrote that inordinate self love is opposed to the love of God. James 2:1-13 talks further about loving others without prejudice. We are to exemplify the same agape love given us by God to others because it is freely given. Agape love refers to the self-sacrificing love of God for humanity, which we are committed to reciprocate towards God and practice towards one another.

Let me illustrate the instinctive need for self-protection from my own experience. I was once on a fast. Usually during these times, my appetite leaves, and once it returns it is typically a sign that I can return to eating. During this fast I remember how sickness and hunger had set in. Well, I inquired of the Lord whether I should stop or continue during this time. However, it was difficult for me to hear His voice because of an instinctive need to self-protect.

To avoid any hardship to my family I began to worry and become fearful. My body was trying to protect itself because it remembered the great hardship to the body during these times of consecration. In truth, self love was what I was dealing with. The self life was trying to preserve itself. I quickly realized this was a battle. This involved the crucifying of the flesh. On the one hand, it was screaming and trying to lure me into its desire, on the other there was the Spirit leading me to persevere.

The Bible says it was the Holy Spirit that led Jesus into the Wilderness to be tempted by the devil. In my case too I noticed that during each moment of prayer led by His Spirit, I felt the Holy Spirit doing a work in me. Once I had a better understanding of what this was, I was equipped to manage the fast. I remember thinking, "Well, food really is not my thing anyway. So, when my appetite returns, I can eat."

However, I failed to take note that eating is one of the appetites of the flesh. We cannot underestimate the works of the flesh with their deeds. I quickly came to understand the issue was not about the food but about yielding completely to His Spirit. At the same time I sensed anxiety setting in, like fear of trauma or of impeding danger, as if trying to avoid something bad from occurring.

This is self love operating at its finest. It was rising up, trying to protect me instead of allowing me to rely on His Spirit. So here was I in a transition from works to being Spirit-led. While I wanted to be in charge of this time in determining when it would end, the Holy Spirit was doing a new thing in me. He wanted to show me how to love Him more through my obedience to Him with no restrictions. He wanted me to wholeheartedly accept His love which is better than my own.

You see, my human love causes me to love out of fear, but His love empowers me to love through fear. Love is not made perfect in that fear, for perfect love casts out all fear (1 John 4:4). My fear blinded me to what God was during at this time. I was so focused on looking to be safe and secure, it robbed me of the ability to be brave in the midst of health challenges. It distracted me from the sure knowledge of who He is and how He planned to work in my life.

Self-Protection

So self love involves self-protection. That is intrinsic to our human nature. But listen to what God has to say about this. "I did not design you to self-protect. You are to seek all that you need from Me and trust Me to meet those needs."

We must love God more than we love ourselves or our own body. We are His body, so what happens to our body happens to Him. This covers more than physical things. We must rid ourselves of the need to defend ourselves even against those who violate, mistreat, or misuse us. We must trust in and seek His protection more than our knee jerk reactions to protect, realizing that self-protection is often in opposition to focusing our trust in Him.

We see this exemplified by Jesus as He always did the will of the Father. He could have come and thrown His weight around, but He chose to demonstrate and reveal the love of His Father instead. He was so certain and stable in Himself, there was no need to bully or intimidate, no need to boast, no need to display His power. He was so complete in His absoluteness there was no need to declare it. The Heavens declare His handiwork, the whole earth is filled with His Glory (see Psalm 19).

What discipline and self-control He displayed before his

rival, Satan, and Man! There was no need to respond. There is no point of time when God will ever exhaust His power as there is no force or rival who can compete with Him. No one can stay His hand, or say to Him, "What are You doing?" This is the God to whom we are to have absolute security in.

To arrive at this place of security you will experience times of testing in the furnace of affliction. At such times it would seem like the hedge is removed – but that seems so only to test our character. Each fiery trial is designed to shape a different facet of you, to make you fit for His Glory. Here you can let go of the burden of trying to hide, rescue or run to safety. You must come to a place of putting your safely in Him through all the obstacle courses of life. Remember, all the challenges, pain and disappointment you face is for a purpose: that you can be made over again. All the pressure is to get it right this time and not mess up again. We will invariably miss the opportunity for growth when at each challenge our goal is to understand the storm, and to run and find shelter from it.

The disciples experienced their own Gethsemane before and after the death of Jesus. At first they were cowering in fear because of the Jews. But when they witnessed the resurrected Christ (and later experienced the Holy Spirit), they learned to love Jesus more than themselves. They experienced what it was like to take on the yoke of Jesus. They loved their lives not unto the death. They gave their lives no value to finish their race. This meant more to them than the saving or protecting of their own lives. Here is where self love vanished, and with it self-protection and the need to hide.

The outward circumstances had not changed: they had to face the same Jews that killed Jesus. But they had come to a place of security and rest that this world could not take away from them. They knew they were His and they understood their mission both through the word, the divine commission to win souls, and the example laid out by Jesus.

What did He reveal to them after His resurrection and final ascension? What transpired during those forty days? Something life-changing. They looked to Jesus. He loved the Father more than Himself and this is the key to doing His will. In this He chose not to protect but to give Himself as a ransom for all. How much more are we to follow this example because He said greater things will we do in His name!

This is when love is made perfect because we love Him more than we love ourselves. It's the only way. How else can we love others if consumed with self love? This is when He has secured us in Him. We must first be His for this to happen because Jesus prayed to the Father, after the washing of the feet of the disciples, "Even as I am in You, keep them also in us."

I had a vision while in prayer one morning. It was more of an inner experience than a sight to the senses. I could see myself somehow lifted above the human heart. It was such a beautiful place. In this vision, I went to a place that was so amazing. All I wanted to do in this sphere was to love Him. Nothing mattered there. Nothing was more important. Life felt so pure and transparent in this place.

Then the Lord spoke to me and said, "It is impossible for the human heart to love Me." I understood in this moment why a new heart is promised and required. I immediately began to ask God for a new heart above human desire, its appetites, and all it entails.

Pride, lust, greed, greed for power did not exist in this place. It was like I was one with Him. This place was so white and clean. It looked like nothing I had ever seen; rather it was a place in the Spirit. I felt this longing for Heaven that I have never felt before. I just wanted to be in His presence. I did not want to go anywhere or be obligated to any task or event. I just wanted more of Him. It was this way for days on end.

The only comparison I can make is the bonding between a mother and her unweaned child. Although the child cannot articulate her needs, she somehow knows when her mother is absent because her cry is frantic. This is her only known security. This is what I experienced for days each time I would leave this secret place. I had this unexplainable longing to be with Him. Tears, fears, and the desire to be in His presence and in His presence only were my constant experience. Just like the child I had no words to express it, but my life reacted when I was absent from it – even the thought of separation.

I now fully understand what was missing in my life. It was not the gaining of authority or power but security in God and Him alone to know I am His. The cares of this world were absent there. You manage as best you can with the affairs of this life; however, there are no attachments to them. All I had was a yearning to enter into His presence once again. I call it the weight of Heaven. It's not a burden. It's more like is a invitation from God to come, enter and remain in this place.

It is the human desires and their lusts that keep us tied to the earthly things. The enemy capitalizes on this to keep us bound to him. He wants to restrict us from desiring or seeking to have a heart after God. We are always seeking for the highest position of power, the latest trends or possessions, sensual gratification, only to be consumed by the desires and cravings of the flesh. All this is heightened by what is in this world.

Just like the child with her mother, we too learn that if Abba Father is there, we are secure. Even if there is a violent storm, we are safe. This is not to be construed that there will be no tests or trials, perils, or hardships. They will come but He will keep us safe in them. Many are the afflictions of the righteous but God has promised to deliver us out of them all (Psalm 34). In every temptation He will rescue us or find a way of escape (1 Corinthians 10:13). That way of escape is in our obedience to Him and His word. His word will remind us of the way to righteousness when we allow the Holy Spirit to purify our hearts.

Obedience does not discount the bountiful supply of grace. For do we not have Jesus' assurance, *"In the world ye shall have tribulation: but be of good cheer; I have overcome the world"*? (John 16:33). We are therefore not to be careless because we are His but to be responsible as we rest in the security of His wings.

Even if you are faced with a health issue, the death of a loved one, a divorce, the loss of a job or emotional hurt and pain, just know that Jesus is there waiting to minister a love so divine and unimaginable. It's a love too beautiful to comprehend. This is who God is and He is waiting to give you this kind of love. There is nothing or no one in this world who can satisfy the unspoken desires in the human heart but God and Him alone. He fashioned the heart, and it is only in Him we can experience the love we desperately seek.

Not Fighting with Flesh and Blood

When we suffer for Christ because of our belief, just know it has nothing to do with the hand of man. It is a spiritual battle.

> *For we wrestle not against flesh and blood but against principalities, against powers, against the rulers of the darkness of this world, against spiritual wickedness in high places* (Ephesians 6:12).

This is because of who you stand for, and that is Jesus. The enemies of the Most-High God, He will deal with. We do not fight with fellow human beings or retaliate when they hurt us. We do not curse those who curse us or take revenge on those who set themselves up as enemies. If we do, we contribute to the enemy's cycle of destruction. Instead, we must forgive and love and make a stand so that His Glory is seen and revealed in us.

Know that the enemy's objective is to hinder the Glory of

God from being revealed in you. He knows that he ultimately cannot stop it from filling the whole earth but if he can get to you, (when you are without your spiritual armor) he can obstruct it through you. He seeks to contaminate the souls of all born again Christians just as he sought to contaminate the pure Messianic line of Christ promised by God. For God told the serpent who represents Satan himself:

> *And I will put enmity between thee and the woman, and between thy seed and her seed; it shall bruise thy head, and thou shalt bruise his heel"* (Genesis 3:15).

God will always protect the seed of the woman, that is, the seed of Christ – all those who are born again in His name. Even so, Satan seeks to contaminate the lives of humans to hinder Christians from becoming true sons of God. You may ask how this is possible? It comes from within us through the works and deeds of the flesh. This he can do by inhibiting the fruit of the Spirit in the lives of His people.

Will you stand up and be part of the remnant that resists every attempt of the enemy?

MY FIRST LOVE

LORD, you are my FIRST LOVE,
my protection, and reward.

Your love is beautiful, secure. Before You
it is safe to be naked, to be unashamed, to
broken, to be vulnerable, to be flawed.

All while tucked away in the security of Your
arms, awaiting the fulfillment of wholeness

– wholeness on standby, waiting only
for absolute surrender.

Even in my worst state, I am forever Your Beloved.
Even in this state of my affliction it ignites and
drives Your love toward me more passionately.

The force behind Your love, the intensity, and fierceness of
this love, it completely engulfs each intricate part of me:

my iniquity, flaws, brokenness, fears, nakedness, and
shame, including my vulnerabilities – known only
by You – heightened by anxiety and fear alone.

You lose my soul from the tumbleweed of
strongholds and entanglements of fear.

You are my Perfect Love, flawed, broken as
I am, yet passionately loved by You.

Perfection and merit are not required for
You, but obedience out of suffering.

The passion behind Your great rescue is simple:
I need you and not that You need me.

In this truth, I clothed my soul in authentic
garments of humility and absolute surrender.

Your desire enwrapped in unconditional love alone
brings to completion Your pursuit of me.

Your love is consistent. It will not be altered; it
cannot be modified, neither will it vary through time
or Eternity. It is IMMUTABLE in its Essence.

I COULDN'T DREAM OF A BETTER LOVE!

Chapter 5

The Fallen Nature

In this chapter we will examine the propensity of man to fall into deception because he is unaware of the spiritual battle at stake. This as we shall see has grave consequences on his present situation and his eternity. There are three major forces that war for our soul: God's will power, Satan's pursuits, and man's volition. We are first going to gain a broad understanding of the Will, the Mind, and the Heart before we dive into the main topic: our fallen nature.

The Will

The will is a faculty of the mind which involves the determination to carry out an action. In philosophy, the will is an important part of the mind, along with reason and understanding. It is central to the field of ethics because of its role in enabling moral action.

The word "will" comes from an Old English word, *wil(l)*, meaning "will, pleasure," and *will(a)*, denoting "the faculty of willing and determining." The will, therefore refers to conscious choice in performing an action or forming a thought. It also denotes a fixed and persistent intent or purpose; hence the saying, "Where there is a will there is a way." "Choice" is the power of forming an intention and using the will to act upon it.

As humans, we are all created with free will and enjoy great liberty as long as we do not allow it to be in bondage to irrational appetites. We see this bondage when Eve made her choice in Genesis 3:6:

> *And when the woman saw that the tree was good*
> *for food, and that it was pleasant to the eyes, and*
> *a tree to be desired to make one wise, she took of*
> *the fruit thereof, and did eat, and gave also unto*
> *her husband with her; and he did eat.*

With free will, we have ability to exercise the power of choice. If we are aware of the powers of choice before us, we become substantially equipped to make the right one.

The Mind

The mind is the organ or seat of consciousness. It performs the higher functions of the human brain, such as cognition, reasoning, willing, and experiencing emotions. It is the organized totality of all mental and psychological processes based their relatedness. The consciousness that originates in the brain is evident in emotion, imagination, memory, perception, thought and choice.

The Heart

The "heart" (Hebrew *lebab/leb*, Greek. *kardia*) is mentioned over one thousand times in the Bible, making it the most common anthropological term in Scripture. It denotes a person's center for both physical and emotional-intellectual-moral activity.

According to the Bible, the heart is also part of man's spiritual makeup. It is the **place where emotions and desires begin**, which drives the will of man towards action. In Christianity, the heart symbolizes the core of our being, from which prayer and moral actions originate. This even explains the word "core," which is derived from the Latin word *cor*, meaning "heart."

The Corrupt Nature

We know that our corrupt nature after the fall is inherent in us all. Let us define and investigate it further. We will need to brace ourselves for hard truths in this chapter; however, the rewards will be great.

From our study of creation in Genesis chapters 1-3, everything God created was good. All things were perfect after their own kind. Adam was formed in the image of God, in righteousness and true holiness. It was the disobedience of our first parents which caused them to fall from their original state of innocence to a state of depravity and we have inherited that nature.

Hence after the fall every succeeding generation was increasingly tainted. By the time we get to Genesis 6 we see an exceedingly corrupt civilization that wanted to build their own society apart from God:

> *And God looked upon the earth, and, behold, it was corrupt; for all flesh had corrupted his way upon the earth* (Genesis 6:12).

Even in our saved state, there is a residue of corruption in us. It is often undetected by us, but it surfaces when our passions get the better of us. Now our appetites and affections take over and we revert to our fallen state of disorder. We love the things in this world far beyond their value and worth. Our love for God does not compare with the objects of our affections. The flesh has spiraled downwards into the inbred corrupt nature.

Remember how man was originally created to know his God, and to love and to serve Him only? Then he was to love his neighbor as himself. However, we are drawn to the total opposite, loving the things of this world and ourselves more than God with little to no intention to love our neighbor as ourselves. We have exchanged humility and meekness for pride.

As David says in his psalm, we become as fools due to our lack of understanding:

> *The fool hath said in his heart, There is no God.*
> *Corrupt are they, and have done abominable in-*
> *iquity: there is none that doeth good. God looked*
> *down from heaven upon the children of men, to see*
> *if there were any that did understand, that did seek*
> *God* (Psalm 53:1-2).

God Himself looks down upon the children of men where all things are naked before Him, and all He sees is the sinfulness of our hearts. Habitual sin becomes iniquity, unrighteous and evil in its practices. It is the consequence of putting aside the fear of God in our eyes. We even claim there is no God so as not to be called to account for our actions. Our bad practices stem from poor principles. Wickedness debases our character through the deceitfulness of sin and contempt for God.

We are no different from the society that the prophet Isaiah laments of:

> *Ah sinful nation, a people laden with iniquity, a seed of evildoers, children that are corrupters: they have forsaken the LORD, they have provoked the Holy One of Israel unto anger, they are gone away backward* (Isaiah 1:6).

The intellect and will of fallen man have become so corrupt, no integrity, no knowledge, or fear of God can be found in him. What kind of will remains in man when sin has enslaved his flesh and has invaded the higher part of the soul? The intellect, will and heart of the whole man have become corrupt.

Jesus was well aware of the deceitfulness of the human condition. For this reason He did not confide in everybody because He knew man (see John 2:24-25). What is it that He knew? Was it the hidden heart of man? Was it the corrupt nature of humankind that caused Him not to put His trust in man? What is it that we are not privy to about ourselves that He is aware of? My prayer is that God will bring light to us as we enter His word so that we are no longer deceived.

We are prone to deception because we do not truly recognize the kind of nature we have inherited from our forefathers. We must come to a full understanding of this so we are prepared to empty the will of all its soulish desires. This happens when the veil that masks our depravity is removed by God's grace. This is when we come to a full perception of the gravity of our sin nature. What will the process look like in the life of one who has true understanding? We will gather answers to each of these questions as we come to a deeper awareness of our sinful tendencies through the Word of God.

We can possess admirable endowments, which may be extraordinary gifts from God. Or they may be highly esteemed by man and have no merit with God. In all this, our inward corruption may not be entirely removed, but only outwardly restrained.

> There is none *righteous, no, not one: There is none that understandeth, there is none that seeketh after God. They are all gone out of the way, they are together become unprofitable; there is none that doeth good, no, no one.*

The flesh is capricious. It strives with all its might against God so that it cannot align with the righteousness of His law. There is nothing in our fallen human nature but flesh. According to Ephesians 4:22, the flesh is "*corrupt according to the deceitful lusts.*" The depraved desires are in the mind itself. All the thoughts that proceed from the human mind are corrupt and perverse.

Let us look at Jeremiah's description of the human heart to highlight a few words:

> *The heart is **deceitful** above all things, and desperately wicked: who can know it? I the Lord search the heart, I try the **reins**, even to give every man according to his ways, and according to the fruit of his doings* (Jeremiah 17:9, emphasis added).

The first word we will define is "deceitful." It means "intended to, or tending to deceive – to lie, mislead, or otherwise hide or distort the truth." The intrinsic condition of the human heart is on display. Even more disappointing is the truth in varying degrees that the core of us is predominantly perverse. The second truth is our desperate, reckless manner of existence, without regard for danger or safety. The third truth is our wickedness, our evil principles or practices in deviating from the moral or divine law in our addiction to vice or sin, and our profligate lifestyle.

From the above portrayal, let me see if I can summarize the condition of the human heart. If our heart has not tried to mislead us, it is only a matter of time before it will. How will it accomplish its task? By concealing or distorting the truth. And as if this was not enough, it passionately moves toward its goal without consideration or calculation of the cost involved: it is reckless!

The second word in the Jeremiah passage is "reins." Here it describes our innermost component – the emotions, feelings, affections, or mind. God deals with each one according to our inward heart, the seat of the affections and passions. He deals with us according to our doings and our ways. This is definitely a good place to pray for the new heart and a new spirit He promised in Ezekiel 36:26.

Romans 3:10-18 describes humankind's perpetual corruption and depravity of nature. Man lacks righteousness with no integrity or purity without sound intelligence from God. To seek Him is the beginning of wisdom. All have gone astray and come to total corruption. There is none that does good. When there is no fear of God, it is vain to look for any good in our nature.

> *As is written, There is none righteous, no, not one:*
> *There is none that understandeth, there is none*
> *that seeketh after God. They are all gone out of*
> *the way, they are together become unprofitable;*
> *there is none that doeth good, no, not one. Their*
> *throat is an open sepulchre; with their tongues they*
> *have used deceit; the poison of asps is under their*

> *lips: Whose mouth is full of cursing and bitterness:*
> *Their feet are swift to shed blood: Destruction and*
> *misery are in their ways: And the way of peace*
> *have they not known: There is no fear of God*
> *before their eyes* (Romans 3:10-18).

Even if there were the highest resemblance of integrity, a corrupt bent will erode it. We cannot esteem any value on any gift or talent that seem praiseworthy in ourselves or in ungodly men. The virtues which deceive us by an empty show of praise in society will be of no value before the judgment seat of God.

The will is enchained as a slave to sin. It cannot pursue goodness. There is a propensity toward sin. Under this bondage it is deprived of the soundness of will but not of a perverse will. Man accepts his fall voluntarily, not by force but by a prejudiced choice of the mind, by it owns passions. He suffers a violence proceeding from his will.

The nature of man's unregenerate intellect and will is described in Jesus' explanation to the religious leader Nicodemus. When he asks about the phenomenon of being "born again," Jesus says to him, *"that which is born of the flesh is flesh and that which is born of the Spirit is spirit"* (John 3:6). Similarly, Paul contrasts flesh and spirit in Romans 8:8, *"To be carnally minded is death. It is enmity against God and is not subject to the law of God, neither can it be."*

Only grace can convert the will. Grace is the cause of our beginning to will proficiently. God does not prepare man's heart merely to do good but initiates our effort to desire Him, to search diligently for Him, and to pursue Him. That which is born of the flesh is flesh and that which is born of the Spirit is spirit. The only escape is conversion to God, through God and owing only to Him.

Ezekiel 36:26-27 reveals the nature of this conversion:

> *A new heart also will I give you, and a new spirit*
> *will I put within you: and I will take away the*
> *stony heart out of your flesh, and I will give you a*
> *heart of flesh. And I will put my spirit within you,*
> *and cause you to walk in my statutes, and ye shall*
> *keep my judgments, and do them.*

Our only escape is the renewing of the mind. For this reason a man must be born again, *"born, not of blood, nor of the will of the flesh, nor of the will of man, but of God"* (John 1:13). Totally renewed, we are imbued with the Spirit through the process of regeneration or rebirth.

So what is our recourse? The grace He so graciously provides, which Philippians 1:1-9 describes:

> *Blessed be the God and Father of our Lord Jesus Christ, who hath blessed us with all spiritual blessings in heavenly places in Christ: According as he hath chosen us in him before the foundation of the world, that we should be holy and without blame before him in love: Having predestinated us unto the adoption of children by Jesus Christ to himself, according to the good pleasure of his will, To the praise of the glory of his grace, wherein he hath made us accepted in the beloved. In whom we have redemption through his blood, the forgiveness of sins, according to the riches of his grace; Wherein he hath abounded toward us in all wisdom and prudence; Having made known unto us the mystery of his will, according to his good pleasure which he hath purposed in himself:*

Only God can begin the conversion of the will. "*Being confident of this very thing, that he which hath begun a good work in you will perform it until the day of Jesus Christ*" (Philippians 1:6) by imputing to us a desire and a love, and by turning, training, and guiding our hearts into righteousness. He works in both our will and ability to do all His good pleasure.

The End of Self

Each waking moment of self-consciousness unloads the unending toil and endless burden of trying to meet the just requirements of righteousness. The unprofitable acts of merit have wearied my soul, and I have discovered all I know I must come to abandon.

For the first time, I have realized I cannot trust the humanistic self I have come to know. All dependency must be upon You. Not apart from You but only in You. You are the only one who died for me.

The flesh did not die, and neither can it, and it wills only to lead and follow hard after a certain path of destruction.

The carnal mind is the absolute enemy of the One who paid the total price for me. It wants to live only in blissful rebellion against Your moral and spiritual laws.

The heart will not die because of its utter desire and passion for deceit, wickedness, and hatred. The core of its quest is to hate.

Not one part of me is committed to the total good
of the well-being of others, my well-being, or the
true Essence of my existence. True dependency
and trust can only be upon You. You are the one in
whom my soul has finally come to trust, the only
one who fights continually and endlessly for me.

You and You alone paid the required penalty. Not my
heart in its wickedness and cruelty, nor my carnal
mind in its contempt for You, not my flesh which
feeds on and seeks only to secure my demise.

You ever live to make intercession for me. You will
not give up on the unformed version of me You
paid for to be made in Your image and likeness.

You began at the beginning. You fought effortlessly
and tirelessly for generations to come to me to
ensure Your Love reached me, woven as a Thread
through all the generations of humanity.

Your Love is so potent, it transcends decades,
dispensations, and ages without diminishing in Quality.

Your love fights for me even when I am unaware,
whether asleep, lost in sin, or in voracious rebellion.

It never stops; it never loses power or Essence. It is all just the same. I am simply Yours, and Your mission has the same Eminence since the futile beginning of sin. Your unconditional love is for humanity.

My soul can finally rest its righteousness in You.

Let us purpose to divest ourselves of the Adam-like nature. To be effective in our efforts of self-denial, it must go all the way back to its futile beginning in each one individually. When the thrust of our desire is to submit to His will, obedience is easy. Can we lay down our self-will and follow Jesus?

> *If any man will come after me, let him deny himself, and take up his cross daily, and follow me. For whosoever will save his life shall lose it: but whosoever will lose his life for my sake, the same shall save it* (Luke 9:23-24).

In the next chapter we will examine what it means to divest ourselves of our Adam-like nature in order to follow Christ.

Chapter 6

The Emptying

Divesting ourselves of the Adam-like nature is akin to emptying ourselves out. It's called *kenosis* in Greek. In this chapter we are going to discuss what the word *kenosis* means in so far as it relates to Christ before His descent to earth. Then we will take a moment to brief ourselves on what it means for us to carry out the process of *kenosis* in ourselves.

Kenosis

Kenosis is mentioned in Philippians 2:7 when Jesus assumed the role of man. In this role He

> ... **emptied Himself** [without renouncing or diminishing His deity, but only temporarily giving up the outward expression of divine equality and His rightful dignity] by assuming the form of a bond-servant, and being made in the likeness of men .... (AMP, emphasis added).

The verb "emptied Himself" comes from the Greek verb *ekenōsen*, which means that Christ "emptied, divested and made void *His* divine nature" – at least in part – at His Incarnation. From here comes the act of *kenosis:* "the empty-ing." In emptying Himself as a man, Jesus divested Himself of His divine glory – though not of His divinity – as an expression of God's humility and servanthood. The stripping away of His majesty and putting on the frailty of our human nature was in itself a humbling act. But more than that, He came as a bond servant of God to serve and minister to man. Christ's *kenosis* is a condescension and self-sacrifice for the redemption and salvation of all humanity.

This act of emptying oneself is the starting point of the Christian concept of *kenosis.* John the Baptist took upon himself the same posture when he said of Jesus: *"He must become greater; I must become* less" (John 3:30). It entailed the yielding of one's personal will and becoming entirely surrendered to God's divine will.

Kenosis for us too is only possible through humility and the desire for union with God. In it we detach ourselves from the world and its passions by an act of disassociation. This can be achieved with the help of the Holy Spirit as we continually call upon His help in denying our own human will of its desires. We then become united to God by grace through His Spirit.

Let us see what Jesus divested Himself of before He put on the attributes of man here on earth.

> But **made himself of no reputation**, and took upon him the form of a servant, and was made in the likeness of men: And being found in fashion as a man, he humbled himself, and became obedient unto death, even the death of the cross (Philippians 2:7, emphasis added).

Christ divested Himself of His Omnipotence, that is, possessing all power. Sovereignty and Omnipotence go hand in hand. To reign sovereignly God must have all power, for He alone is Almighty. He alone possesses what no creature can have: an inexhaustible abundance of power, a power that is absolute. As the self-existent Creator, He is the source of all power. It is true He delegates power to His creatures, but being self-sufficient, He cannot relinquish any of His perfections, including His power. He gives but He does not *give away*. All that He gives remains His own and returns to Him again.

> For by him were all things created, that are in heaven, and that are in earth, visible and invisible, whether they be thrones, or dominions, or

> *principalities, or powers: all things were created by*
> *him, and for him (Colossians 1:16).*

He must remain forever what He has forever been: the Lord God Omnipotent. He has at His command all the power in the universe. He does as He wills and nothing is too difficult when He has absolute power. All His acts are effortless: He expends no energy that needs replenishing. His self-sufficiency makes it unnecessary for Him to look outside of Himself to renew His strength.

Now look at what happened when Jesus took on the form of man, made after the flesh and born of a woman through the power of the Holy Spirit. When He said, "Prepare me a body to do Your will" (Hebrews 10:5), the Holy Spirit over-shadowed Mary and impregnated her with a spiritual seed. The Bible says that by the seed of the woman the promise would come. It was the seed of a woman that brought forth the Word into existence. So the Word was made flesh and dwelt bodily among us. He was completely God as if He were not man, and completely man as if He were not God.

In summary, Christ divested Himself of His ability and power to do anything without His Father's approval. All ability He had was through the enabling of the Holy Spirit. He accepted the limitations of His human role the same way everything He has created knows its limits. The waves have boundaries to their reach. The earth is governed and defined within boundaries set for it by God during creation. Even Satan has parameters to limit his ability and power. Only God has absolute control over all things created.

Theosis

Though the word *theosis* is not found in the Bible, it is used by Bible scholars to denote a transformative process towards likeness to or union with God.

As a process of transformation, *theosis* is brought about by both the purification of mind and body and *theoria*, "illumination" with the "vision" of God. Hence *theosis* becomes the purpose of human life and can only be achieved through the grace of God and our cooperation.

However the principle that "God is One" sets an absolute limit to the extent of *theosis* because it is not possible for any created being of his very nature to become as God, or even a necessary part of God. A created being cannot become Jesus Christ, the Holy Spirit or the Father of the Trinity. Creatures cannot become God in their transcendent essence (*ousia*), or a kind of hyper-being.

Nonetheless, this limited aspiration of man does give

hope to the "deification" of human nature provided by the Incarnation of Jesus. This is what gives man his Christ-like character. Let us aspire to become the image of the one whole God, bearing nothing earthly in ourselves, so that we may be in communion with God. For He who became man though without sin (Hebrews 4:15) will divinize human nature without changing it into the Divine Nature and will raise it up for His Own sake. This is what Paul teaches when he says, *"that in the ages to come he might display the overflowing richness of His grace"* (Ephesians 2:7).

Through *theoria* (illumination with or direct experience of the Triune God), human beings come to know and experience what it means to be fully human. This means that God shares with us through our communion with Christ all that He is in knowledge, righteousness, and holiness. Just as God became human in all ways except sin, He will enable humans to be "holy" or "saintly" in all ways except His Divine Essence.

But following the only true and stedfast Teacher, the Word of God, our Lord Jesus Christ, who did, through His transcendent love, become what we are, that He might bring us to be even what He is Himself.

Here is a picture of the restoration of all humanity to its fullest potential in Christ. Just as the Son of God took to Himself a human nature born of a woman and subjected

Himself to human suffering due to sin (while remaining in His God-unchanged nature unblemished by sin), the natures of God and man in Christ are not two persons but one. This is a union offered in Christ to all of humanity in principle. So, the holy God and sinful humanity are reconciled in principle in the one sinless man, Jesus Christ.

That is why the psalmist David could wonder:

> *What is man, that thou art mindful of him? and the son of man, that thou visitest him? For thou hast made him a little lower than the angels, and hast crowned him with glory and honour* (Psalm 8:4-5).

Theosis begins with the struggles of this life, increases in the experience of the knowledge of God, and is finally consummated in the end-time resurrection of the believer (1 Corinthians 15:51-54). Without the struggle and the practice, there is no real faith. As the Apostle James tells us, faith must lead to action, and without action faith is dead. One must unite one's will, thoughts, and actions to God's will, thoughts, and actions. A person must fashion his life to be a mirror or true likeness of God. Just as God and humanity are more than a similarity in Christ but rather a true union, the Christian life is more than mere imitation but a union with the life of God Himself. In other words, the one who is working out his salvation is united with God at work within him both to will and to do His pleasure (Philippians 2:13).

Every man in whom Christ lives has the potential to partake of the glory of Christ. Here the victory of God over fear, sin, and death, accomplished in the crucifixion and resurrection of Jesus Christ, is made manifest in the believer forever.

In the pursuit of *theosis*, it is important to cultivate the "prayer of the heart," and the prayer that never ceases, as Paul exhorts us to do in 1 Thessalonians 5:17. No one can reach *theosis* without impeccable Christian living, crowned by the faithful, warm, and silent, continuous Prayer of the Heart.

In this deification process, the "doer" is the Holy Spirit and the recipient is the human being who joins his will to His and receives this transforming grace. In so doing, he becomes filled with the Light of the Holy Spirit to the degree that he opens himself to it by loving cooperation in practice and prayer. This cooperation between God and Man expresses unity in the complementary role of the created and the Creator. The Holy Spirit plays a key role in all this as the progressive in-filling of the Spirit leads to progressive knowledge of God. This we shall see in the next few chapters as we progress from living spirits to living in the glory to being endued with power.

Chapter 7

Living Spirits

There is a life stirring inside every living creature: this is the essence of something living. That essence is called the *ruach* or breath. The *ruach* emanates from the Holy Spirit as we see in Genesis 1:2: "*And the earth was without form, and void; and darkness was upon the face of the deep. And the Spirit of God moved upon the face of the waters.*"

Let us return to certain key verses in Genesis to consider the type of life that God offers to man.

> *And the LORD God **formed man** of the dust of the ground, and **breathed into his nostrils the breath of life**; and man became **a living soul** (Genesis 2:7, emphasis added).*

> *And God said, Let us make man **in our image**, after our likeness: and let them have dominion over the fish of the sea, and over the fowl of the air, and over the cattle, and over all the earth, and over every creeping thing that creepeth upon the earth (Genesis 1:26, emphasis added).*

Now in man there is the material body as well as are two

non-material essences that make a human alive. They are the soul and the spirit, breathed upon by the *ruach* that gives the body life and makes us living souls.

All living souls enjoy a life on earth but not all living souls will enjoy heaven with their Creator. How the human spirit responds to the breath of the Spirit of God is crucial because the outcome will determine the place where we will spend our eternity.

The righteous in Christ and the unrighteous who deny Christ will ultimately take separate paths. Only the righteous will enter into eternal life with Christ forever. On the other hand, the unrighteous receive only one earthly life but, as a consequence of their choice, they ultimately forfeit eternal life with Christ. This contrast is clearly depicted in Revelation 20 and 22.

> *And I saw a great white throne, and him sat on it, from whose face the earth and the heaven fled away: and the books were opened: and another book was opened, which is the book of life: and the dead were judged out of those things which were written in the books, according to their works. And the sea gave up the dead which were in it: and death and hell delivered up the dead which were in*

them: and they were judged every man according to their works. And death and hell were cast into the lake of fire. This is the second death. And whosoever was not found written in the book of life was cast into the lake of fire (Revelation 20:11-15).

Those who intentionally reject Christ remain in their sin forever. They have no more recourse to God's mercy and are forever barred from entering the Kingdom.

He that is unjust, let him be unjust still: and he which is filthy, let him be filthy still: and he that is righteous, let him be righteous still: and he that is holy, let him be holy still. And behold, I come quickly, and my reward is with me, to give every man according as his work shall be. I am Alpha and Omega, the beginning and the end, the first and the last. Blessed are they that do his commandments, that they may have right to the tree of life, and nay enter in through the gates in the city. For without are dogs, and sorcerers and whoemongers and murders and idolaters and whosoever loveth and maketh a lie (Revelation 22:11-15).

So as John 17:3 explains, eternal life is vested in the

knowledge of the true God and His Christ.: *"And this is life eternal, that they might know thee the only true God, and Jesus Christ, whom thou hast sent."* Those that have made that investment have the right to the second life and may partake of the Tree of Eternal Life.

Once you have been imbued with the character of God, you begin to show forth His glory as we shall see in a moment.

The Glory

The glory of God is the beauty of His Spirit, the essence of who He is. It is what emanates from His Character. This Glory can crown man or fill the earth. While it can be seen in the beauty of the material world around us, the Glory of God is eternal, transcending time. Manifested in all His attributes together, it will never pass away. Although we have a glimpse of His glory within man and in the earth, it is just a glimpse.

In Old Testament times, no one could see the glory of God and hope to remain alive. Nevertheless He gave Moses, hidden in the cleft of the rock, the chance to see His partial glory as He passed by:

> *And he said, I will make all my goodness pass before thee, and I will proclaim the name of the LORD before thee; and will be gracious to whom I*

*will be gracious, and will shew mercy on whom I will shew mercy. And he said, Thou canst not see my face: for there shall no man see me, and live. And the LORD said, Behold, there is a place by me, and thou shalt stand upon a rock: And it shall come to pass, **while my glory passeth by**, that I will put thee in a clift of the rock, and will cover thee with my hand while I pass by: And I will take away mine hand, and thou shalt see my back parts: but my face shall not be seen* (Exodus 33:19-23, emphasis added).

Before He went to the cross, Jesus prayed to the Father that the same unity between Father and Son be given to His people. He told the Father that the same glory given to Him that had been bestowed on us:

As thou hast sent me into the world, even so have I also sent them into the world. And for their sakes I sanctify myself, that they also might be sanctified through the truth. Neither pray I for these alone, but for them also which shall believe on me through their word; That they all may be one; as thou, Father, art in me, and I in thee, that they also may

*be one in us: that the world may believe that thou
hast sent me.*

*And **the glory** which thou gavest me I have given
them; that they may be one, even as we are one: I
in them, and thou in me, that they may be made
perfect in one; and that the world may know that
thou hast sent me, and hast loved them, as thou
hast loved me* (John 17:18-23, emphasis added).

When the glory of God falls upon man, he can do great
exploits in Jesus' name:

*Even every one that is called by my name: for I
have created him for my glory, I have formed him;
yea, I have made him* (Isaiah 43:7).

Heaven is the place where the Glory of God resides as
the psalmist says, *"Thou shalt guide me with thy counsel, and
afterward receive me to glory"* (Psalm 73:24). At the same time
His glory as displayed in nature speaks to man and draws us
intuitively to Him.

*The heavens declare the glory of God; and the
firmament sheweth his handywork. Day unto
day uttereth speech, and night unto night sheweth*

knowledge. There is no speech nor language, where their voice is not heard. Their line is gone out through all the earth, and their words to the end of the world. In them hath he set a tabernacle for the sun (Psalm 19:1-4).

His glory is therefore constantly being displayed in the universe. Just as we see it manifested in the heavens, we see it in humanity through our acts of goodness, kindness and love. All come from God and all go back to Him. We find the source of all beauty in Jesus. He came that He might reveal the essence and nature of God the Father.

Who *being the brightness of his glory, and the express image of his person, and upholding all things by the word of his power, when he had by himself purged our sins, sat down on the right hand of the Majesty on high ...*" (Hebrews 1:3).

Now we shall look at how we can operate in His power.

Chapter 8

Entrusted with Power

Before anything can be entrusted with power there is always a stage of evaluation. This is necessary to try the quality of a thing and be assured of its performance or reliability before putting it to widespread use.

This is what Jesus experienced in the Wilderness during His time of testing. During His encounter with the devil, He was examined to see if His character met the standards of a righteous God. The Bible says He was "led into the wilderness" rather than tempted by Satan to venture there. The wilderness was therefore the arena of evaluation. Notice that prior to this Jesus was full of the Spirit of God. He had the Glory of God but He did not receive the Power to serve until after the testing; thus He emerged from the wilderness full of the power of the Spirit.

So Jesus had to undergo a validation process before His public ministry began. He was anointed by John the Baptist, and scrutinized by the devil before He was endued with nine gifts of the Spirit at His discretion. It must be emphasized that whether He gives us one or all of the nine gifts, they are intended more for service than for individual use.

Before His ascension to Heaven, Jesus instructed His disciples to preach the gospel, to heal the sick and to cast out devils, and He prepared them for the coming of the Holy Spirit in a short time. Forty days later the Holy Spirit fell upon them and the first evidence that they were filled was their speaking in unknown tongues, which is one of the nine gifts (Acts 2:24).

Let us take a moment to review these gifts in 1 Corinthians 12 and how we are to use them.

The Nine Gifts of the Spirit

The Word of Knowledge. This gift of the Holy Spirit is having knowledge about something that you have no means to know based on your human intelligence.

The Word of Wisdom. Working with the word of knowledge, the word of wisdom gives you the ability and understanding of how to apply the word of knowledge.

The Gift of Prophecy. This gift is a direct Word from the Lord to edify, encourage and comfort the body of Christ. The scripture exhorts us "to especially desire" the gift of prophecy.

The Gift of Faith. This gift grows as we walk with the Lord trusting in His mercy and goodness. Note that faith is both a fruit of the Spirit (Galatians 5:22-23) and a gift. As a fruit it is a lifestyle of faith starting with our initial faith that saves us. The gift of faith is a sudden surge of faith, which empowers us to move to new levels to do miracles and wonders in His name.

The Gifts of Healings. Notice that the scripture says "gifts" in the plural. There are diverse kinds of healings that the Spirit will do through us, implying physical healing, emotional and inner healing. These gifts equip you in numerous ways to access healing for yourself or be an anointed vessel for the healing of others.

The Working of Miracles. We see this gift in operation throughout the Bible, from Moses parting the Red Sea to Jesus feeding the five thousand. God is still in the business of working miracles. Like the word of knowledge, this spiritual gift is manifested, not by human effort, but by the power of the Holy Spirit. It edifies and delivers others.

The Discerning of Spirits. This gift equips the recipient with the ability to see or sense evil spirits operating in someone's life. The Holy Spirit pulls back the curtains to expose the demonic realm so that the person can experience deliverance from their bondage.

Different Kinds of Tongues. This gift is the supernatural

ability to speak and pray in a language that in not known to them. Tongues can be used in your personal prayer when speaking directly to God. Or it can be used corporately when a group prays in tongues, or it can be released to another believer or the whole body as a prophetic utterance in the assembly (1 Corinthians 14:2, 13-14). In public settings tongues should always be followed by the next gift – the interpretation of tongues.

Interpretation of Tongues. This gift is to interpret the tongues spoken by another in the language of the hearer(s). This can either be for yourself (see 1 Corinthians 14:13-14) or for the Church (see 1 Corinthians 14:27-28).

Ambassadors for Christ

As the sent-out ones of Christ, we are ambassadors of the Kingdom of God. We operate and walk above the world's system, not needing to seek its approval, acceptance, or authority. If we seek the world's approval, how can we speak to them with authority?

When you operate from the Kingdom of God, all of Heaven's resources and power are at your disposal. Elijah exercised his authority when he locked the heavens for three and a half years during the reign of King Ahab. Married to

Jezebel, Ahab was one of the wickedest kings of that era. Nevertheless Elijah was undaunted by this when he declared "It will not rain except by my word," and God honored the prophet's words and held back the rain (1 Kings 17).

We also see the miraculous protection of God at work when Paul was bitten by a deadly snake on the island of Malta. While the native people were waiting to see Paul drop dead at any moment, Paul merely shook the creature off with his hand, completely unharmed (Acts 28:3).

We see divine protection when the three Hebrew boys were thrown into the fiery furnace during the reign of Nebuchadnezzar and with Daniel in the lion's den in the reign of Darius; all came out unscathed (Daniel 3:8-25; 6:16-23). God used Elisha to single-handedly defeat the Aramean army and heard his request when he prayed to the Lord to make them blind and subsequently prayed to restore their sight (2 Kings 6:18-23).

And as He was faithful in the past, so is He always faithful to us. He gives us the courage we need so we can do all that He bestows upon us. He also strengthens us with ability to endure hard and challenging times.

The Pearl of Immense Value

So we are to be emptied to be filled again. Remember, He cannot fill vessels that are already full. We must be empty of all the corrupt human nature and then filled with all the Glory of God that He bestows on His children. We must let go of all the habits and pursuits enjoined to the self-life. As we empty ourselves daily, we accept our cross daily. We are no longer loyal to the flesh that keeps us bound to inbred sin and opens us to all the advances of the devil.

Jesus teaches how to live a simple life in Him, a life without the human theatrics that keep us bound to the flesh.

> *Come unto me, all ye that labour and are heavy laden, and I will give you rest. Take my yoke upon you, and learn of me; for I am meek and lowly in heart: and ye shall find rest unto your souls. For my yoke is easy, and my burden is light* (Matthew 11:28-30).

Outside of our salvation and Eternity with Jesus, sonship is our greatest reward. To be crowned with His Glory and His Honor is the highest place of honor for all humankind and angels alike.

However, the process of surrender in the mortification of

the flesh is not an easy one. Our flesh will naturally do battle against the Spirit. It will take great perseverance to summon our will to surrender at each point of testing.

When I left Oklahoma, I sold my house and packed everything I owned in the hope of finding rest, security, and peace. Thinking that the worst was behind me, I had no idea my greatest battles were ahead. I had no idea of the cost of a surrendered life. I did not know what to expect and what it truly entailed. Somehow, I thought and believed I was ready and willing to pay the cost with little understanding of the real cost – the kind of surrender truly poured out to Him for His good pleasure. I did not know the difference between being offered up and following a recommendation by God like Job.

As I look back on the seasons of life during this time. I can see how God used them to shape me and to make me anew. He began to tear down and to demolish erroneous belief systems about Him and His Word. He came after all the fallacies and untruths. He came through the trials, situations, and short comings, including my mistakes and mishaps. All this processing was necessary to make me into the image of Jesus.

On the outside looking in we really do believe we are okay and there's nothing major that needs fixing. However, it's only when God begins to tear down and pull back the veil of our hearts that we come to a true discovery of what is hidden. I have discovered each trial in life will come either to tear down, or to build and fortify. If we have some impediment, then to root up and then build is in order. If there is insufficient strength, then there's the need to fortify. We must therefore pay attention to our trials, testings, and temptations. God is trying to do a work in us; but we must be sensitive to His processing. We must trust that He alone is Sovereign and knows the inner workings of the human heart.

So temptations bring to the surface all that is inside of us. When that is revealed, we can identify its nature and offer it up to God. We have to replace it with the fruit of His Spirit. Once this process is complete, there will be another test for Him to evaluate His product. This also gives us an opportunity to decide if we will agree with the work He began in us or if we will revert to our old nature. I call this His compliance measure. We must agree with Him and become the work He has completed in us. If we agree and conform, this new character trait is now our identity. If we do not, then the process will begin again at some point or another.

As for me, His work was to instill fundamental truths about who He is, to get me back to the simple truths of the Bible. What good is great revelation when we are entrapped in bondage? No, I had to chose to live for Him more than my innate desire to live for myself. He had to show me the path to get there. He had to allow me to understand the purpose of each hurt pain or disappointment in life so that I could come to a right understanding of His plan for my life. He had to reveal to me what was hidden and still intact within my human nature so He could strengthen me to weather the times of testing and hardship. The hardships do not go away automatically but in Him we are to be strengthened to be more than conquerors. We are to be conformed to the nature of Christ, and fortified with the armor He provides.

Lord, I pray You bring us to a place of absolute surrender to Your will and ways. Teach us to properly exercise our power of choice. Help us to know what is required for each temptation, test, or trial. It is here we begin to live, to move and have our being in You, loving no part of the world. Enable us to make all our choices and decisions in You and none apart from You. Let all things be done for Your Glory.

Will you make Him your Pearl of Great Price and will you be His Pearl of Great Price too?

References

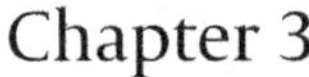

Chapter 3

Dake Annotated Reference Bible, Finis Jennings Dake, Dake Publishing, (1963)

God's Plan for Man, Finis Jennings Dake, Dake Publishing, (1949)

Chapter 5

VA. (n.d.) *Farlex Partner Medical Dictionary.* (2012). Retrieved November 11 2022 from http://medical-dictionary.thefreedictionary.com/VA

Miller-Keane and O'Toole, M. (2003). *Miller-Keane Encyclopedia & Dictionary of Medicine, Nursing & Allied Health.* Revised Reprint, 7th Edition, Elsevier, Amsterdam.

Every Thing Proceeding from the Corrupt Nature of Man Damnable. (n.d.). https://biblehub.com/library/calvin/the_institutes_of_the_christian_religion/chapter_3_every_thing_proceeding.htm

Chapter 6

Kenosis. Wikipedia. https://en.wikipedia.org/wiki/Kenosis

Theosis. (Eastern Christian theology). Wikipedia. https://en.wikipedia.org/wiki/Theosis_(Eastern_Christian_theology)

Chapter 7

The Glory. (n.d.) https://www.gotquestions.org/glory-of-God.html

Chapter 8

Curt Landry Ministries. (2020). What Are the 9 Gifts of the Holy Spirit? https://www.curtlandry.com/9-gifts-of-the-holy-spirit/

Books by Tabitha Henton Lamb

Weathering Life's Storms

Equipping Yourself to Face the Challenges

Understanding God's Plan

Re-evaluating Your Relationship With God

The Purpose of Pain

How God Uses Pain to Strengthen Your Resolve

Enriching the Immortal Soul

A Journey Towards God

Available wherever books are sold.

Author Contact Information

You may contact the author at:

2008 Airline Drive, Ste. 300 #202

Bossier City, LA 71111

Email: admin@thlministries.org

www.thlministries.org

phone: 318-918-9248

Made in the USA
Monee, IL
07 July 2026

56548203R00069